PRAYER MANUAL

By Gene Moody

Deliverance Ministries
Gene B. Moody
14930 Jefferson Highway
Baton Rouge, LA 70817-5217
www.genemoody.com

Telephone: (225) 755-8870
Fax: (225) 755-6120

PRAYER MANUAL

TABLE OF CONTENTS – OVERVIEW

PRAYER MANUAL

TABLE OF CONTENTS - DETAILED

SECTION 1 - SPIRITUAL WARFARE COMBINATION PRAYERS

WE ASK IN THE NAME OF JESUS CHRIST, LORD, MASTER AND SAVIOR.

CONTENTS

SPIRITUAL WARFARE GENERAL
American Civil Liberties Union

DEAR HEAVENLY AND GRACIOUS FATHER, we pray for everyone associated with American Civil Liberties Union to come into THE SAVING KNOWLEDGE OF JESUS CHRIST. We bind the principalities, powers, rulers of darkness of this world, spiritual wickedness in high places and kingdom of evil.

Spiritual Warfare Personal
Gene's Ministry

1. To be a spiritual and physical eunuch.
2. To be an intercessor.
3. To be sensitive to and led by THE HOLY SPIRIT.
4. That you would do great works through me.
5. That the long sword that you have given me will go through the world and destroy the enemies of GOD.

6.   That through Byron's and Earline's deaths the thoughts of many hearts will be revealed.

7.   That the ministry will increase.

8.   To use my life and resources in the battle against Satan and his kingdom.

9.   To do as much damage to the Kingdom of Satan as I can.

10.   To have GOD set my ministry schedule.

11.   To train an army for GOD, and Christians to do deliverance and healing.

12.   To break curses on the ministry.

Gene's Personal Life

1.   For the needs of our family.

2.   For the proper relationship with my relatives.

3.   That I would be a Light for GOD in my community.

4.   For every thing that pertains to me: home, farm, community, parish, city, state, nation and world.

5.   For everyone that I have a relationship with.

6.   For divine health: mental, physical, spiritual and material.

7.   To have GOD set my personal schedule.

8.   To break curses on my personal life.

Nathan, Marie, Nat, Natasha And Rachel

1.   That they would follow the leadership of THE HOLY SPIRIT.

2.   That they would have divine health: mental, physical, spiritual and material.

3.   For Nathan for healing of the pinched nerve in his back and for him to be able to address the negative part of life.

4.   For Marie for healing of her body and allergy to poison ivy.

5.   For Nat for healing of his digestive system and for him to learn how to eat properly.

6.   For Natasha that she will not try to control others.

7.   For Analytical and Environmental Testing for a proper cash flow.

8.   For deliverance for Nathan, Marie, Nat, Natasha and Rachel.

9.   To break curses on Nathan, Marie, Nat, Natasha and Rachel.

Moody's/Hughes'- Chauncey's/Wilson's - Levy's/Hendrey's - Hostetler's/Kalkan's

1.   For the Chauncey families: Beverly, Donald and Carolyn, Wilburn and Gwen, Saralene and their descendants.

2.   For the Levy family relatives to come into a saving knowledge of JESUS CHRIST.

3.   To break curses on Moody's and Hughes', Chauncey's and Wilson's, Levy's and Hendrey's, Hostetler's and Kalkan's.

Other People

1.   For those who are involved in deliverance.

2.   For everyone who has written us and has requested prayer from Earline and me.

3.   For those that I have a relationship with in the ministry.

4.   For people in foreign countries that I support: Bahamas, Canada, England,

Ghana, India, Malawi, Nigeria, Philippines, Romania, Scotland and other countries.

5. For the packages mailed around the world that they would arrive safely at their destinations.
6. For the information that we have sent around the world that THE HOLY SPIRIT will use it to further the KINGDOM OF GOD.
7. For the Deliverance Manuals that have been distributed that THE HOLY SPIRIT would teach people how to do deliverance.
8. For everyone that Earline and I have prayed for.
9. For organizations and people that have requested a **Deliverance Manual**, are in the ministry of deliverance and healing, and we have supported financially and with our time. Those that are ministering to the persecuted Christians, trying to save children from abortions, leading us in fasting and prayer, and Messianic Jewish (Christian).
10. To break curses on the people that I am associated with.

Thanksgiving

Thank You for meeting every need out of your RICHES IN GLORY THROUGH JESUS CHRIST (Phil. 4:19). **Thank You for every blessing known and unknown, and for showering down blessings so great that we can not receive them** (Mal. 3:10). DEAR HEAVENLY AND GRACIOUS FATHER, thank You for divine health: mental, physical, spiritual and material. Thank You for the restoration of our bodies. Thank You for every provision.

At The Breakfast Table

We confess that this is the day that the LORD has made; We will rejoice and be glad in it (Psa. 118:24). For GOD has not given us a spirit of fear but of power, love and a sound mind (II Tim. 1:7). He that is in us is greater than he that is in the world (I John 4:4). If GOD be for us, who can be against us? (Rom. 8:31). You have given us power over all the power of the enemy and we intend to exercise it by the leadership of THE HOLY SPIRIT (Luke 10:19).

DEAR HEAVENLY AND GRACIOUS FATHER, thank You for a good day, for protecting us against powers, principalities, evil forces in this world and spiritual wickedness in high places. We apply THE BLOOD OF JESUS CHRIST over and bind Satan away from Nathan, Marie, Nat, Natasha and Rachel, Chapel on the Campus, Analytical And Environmental Testing, and everything that we have part in. Send your angels to minister unto us, place a ring of HOLY GHOST FIRE around us and cover us with Your Blood.

We pray for the United States of America and Israel, Christians and Jews, and churches that worship JESUS CHRIST in spirit and truth. We ask for courage, understanding, wisdom and strength. We pray especially for the leaders and ask a double portion for our families. We ask divine favor with You in accordance with THE HOLY WORD OF GOD, with each other and those we come into contact with today.

We ask that You lead, guide, direct and protect us. Let us walk in your perfect will; we yield ourselves to you today. We thank You for our food, clothing and shelter, and for everything that You have done for us known and unknown. We ask you to bless this food to our bodies, purify and cleanse it so that our temples will be fit for THE HOLY SPIRIT to reside in. We ask GOD to circumcise our thoughts.

For The Day
We thank You for power and authority over the enemy, and the right to use THE NAME OF JESUS CHRIST. DEAR HEAVENLY AND GRACIOUS FATHER, we ask you to forgive us of our sins, teach us and show us so that we will be pleasing in your sight. We pray for ourselves, Nathan, Marie, Nat, Natasha and Rachel, this day and the leadership of THE HOLY SPIRIT. We thank You for each other, this day and most of all for You. We pray for our relatives, friends, and Christian brothers and sisters. We pray for those who labor in the field of deliverance, for their families, churches and ministries that You would give them a triple-fold portion of courage, understanding, wisdom and strength.

We pray for THE ARMY OF THE LORD that it would grow strong and mighty, and be valiant and do exploits in THE NAME OF JESUS CHRIST. We pray that deliverance would come to the forefront of Christianity. We pray for the five-fold ministry, those that we have ministered to, and their families, churches and ministries that they would follow THE LORD. We pray for men and women everywhere that they would come into the saving knowledge of JESUS CHRIST. We pray Your Blessings on these.

In A Restaurant
DEAR HEAVENLY AND GRACIOUS FATHER, thank You for this food. Bless, purify and cleanse it so that we can be fit temples for THE HOLY SPIRIT to reside in. We break any curses on it and eat it with thanksgiving.

The Lord's Prayer
Our FATHER which art in Heaven, Hallowed be thy name. Thy kingdom come, Thy will be done in earth, as it is in Heaven. Give us this day our daily bread. <u>AND FORGIVE US OUR DEBTS, AS WE FORGIVE OUR DEBTORS</u>. And lead us not into temptation, but deliver us from evil: For thine is the kingdom and the power, and the glory, for ever. (Matt. 6:9-13).

Thanksgiving
Thank You for meeting every need out of your RICHES IN GLORY THROUGH JESUS CHRIST (Phil. 4:19). **Thank You for every blessing known and unknown, and for showering down blessings so great that we can not receive them** (Mal. 3:10). DEAR HEAVENLY AND GRACIOUS FATHER, thank You for divine health: mental, physical, spiritual and material. Thank You for the restoration of our bodies. Thank You for every provision.

At The Breakfast Table

We confess that this is the day that the LORD has made; We will rejoice and be glad in it (Psa. 118:24). For GOD has not given us a spirit of fear but of power, love and a sound mind (II Tim. 1:7). He that is in us is greater than he that is in the world (I John 4:4). If GOD be for us, who can be against us? (Rom. 8:31). You have given us power over all the power of the enemy and we intend to exercise it by the leadership of THE HOLY SPIRIT (Luke 10:19).

DEAR HEAVENLY AND GRACIOUS FATHER, thank You for a good day, for protecting us against powers, principalities, evil forces in this world and spiritual wickedness in high places. We apply THE BLOOD OF JESUS CHRIST over and bind Satan away from Nathan, Marie, Nat, Natasha and Rachel, Chapel on the Campus, Analytical And Environmental Testing, and everything that we have part in. Send your angels to minister unto us, place a ring of HOLY GHOST FIRE around us and cover us with Your Blood.

We pray for the United States of America and Israel, Christians and Jews, and churches that worship JESUS CHRIST in spirit and truth. We ask for courage, understanding, wisdom and strength. We pray especially for the leaders and ask a double portion for our families. We ask divine favor with You in accordance with THE HOLY WORD OF GOD, with each other and those we come into contact with today.

We ask that You lead, guide, direct and protect us. Let us walk in your perfect will; we yield ourselves to you today. We thank You for our food, clothing and shelter, and for everything that You have done for us known and unknown. We ask you to bless this food to our bodies, purify and cleanse it so that our temples will be fit for THE HOLY SPIRIT to reside in. We ask GOD to circumcise our thoughts.

For The Day

We thank You for power and authority over the enemy, and the right to use THE NAME OF JESUS CHRIST. DEAR HEAVENLY AND GRACIOUS FATHER, we ask you to forgive us of our sins, teach us and show us so that we will be pleasing in your sight. We pray for ourselves, Nathan, Marie, Nat, Natasha and Rachel, this day and the leadership of THE HOLY SPIRIT. We thank You for each other, this day and most of all for You. We pray for our relatives, friends, and Christian brothers and sisters. We pray for those who labor in the field of deliverance, for their families, churches and ministries that You would give them a triple-fold portion of courage, understanding, wisdom and strength.

We pray for THE ARMY OF THE LORD that it would grow strong and mighty, and be valiant and do exploits in THE NAME OF JESUS CHRIST. We pray that deliverance would come to the forefront of Christianity. We pray for the five-fold ministry, those that we have ministered to, and their families, churches and ministries that they would follow THE LORD. We pray for men and women everywhere that they would come into the saving knowledge of JESUS CHRIST. We pray Your Blessings on these.

In A Restaurant

DEAR HEAVENLY AND GRACIOUS FATHER, thank You for this food. Bless, purify and cleanse it so that we can be fit temples for THE HOLY SPIRIT to reside in. We break any curses on it and eat it with thanksgiving.

The Lord's

Our FATHER which art in Heaven, Hallowed be thy name. Thy kingdom come, Thy will be done in earth, as it is in Heaven. Give us this day our daily bread. AND FORGIVE US OUR DEBTS, AS WE FORGIVE OUR DEBTORS. And lead us not into temptation, but deliver us from evil: For thine is the kingdom and the power, and the glory, for ever. (Matt. 6:9-13).

SPIRITUAL WARFARE PORTIONS
Agreement With Others

According to Matt. 18:18 - 20, I agree with my Christian brothers and sisters around the world, as they agree with God the father, God the son, God the Holy Spirit, God's Holy Bible. We stand united in God against the forces of evil.

For Protection

Only THE FATHER, SON and HOLY SPIRIT can protect us. We thank You for this protection. We ask that you send our personal angels and reinforcements from the Third Heaven of legions of angels to place an impenetrable shield around us so that we will be protected from evil. We can not protect ourselves.

For Enemies

We pray for our enemies who are doing evil that they will get saved and JESUS CHRIST will become their LORD, MASTER AND SAVIOR. We send our blessings and love to them as a weapon to break down the barriers against JESUS CHRIST. May GOD bring them into salvation and truth, bless them with spiritual blessings and meet their needs out of His Riches in Glory.

For Government

We ask that GOD stretch forth CHRIST's authority over the nations and their rulers. We make supplications, prayers, intercessions, and giving of thanks for all men. We ask that GOD deal with bad government so that men can be saved. We pray for good government, and ask GOD to answer according to His will. We ask that GOD exercise his power to bring about the necessary changes.

For America

We plead for forgiveness for innocent blood of millions of babies offered in sacrifice to Molech, Baal, Chemosh, Milcom, Shamash and others (the Gods of child sacrifice). We humble ourselves in repentance. We grieve over sins of ourselves and nation. We ask you to forgive us and nation cursed for loving and serving money and material things more than you. Help us to turn from wicked ways and seek your face. Forgive us and The Church for allowing liberalism to creep into our hearts and destroy the testimony of The Church.

Innocent blood has covered America and we surely deserve your judgement. Shake America and show our nation what you think about sins. Shake the churches and show Christians how they have failed America and You. We pray for everyone connected to this nation that they will turn from sin and come back to GOD. Show our churches how they are responsible for the spiritual state of the nation; Christians - the spiritual state of the world.

We pray that GOD will be THE LORD of America, expose evil to the world, unravel the interlocking of evil groups, bring confusion in their midst, defeat their plans and loose the heavenly powers against our enemies who want to destroy America. We command the powers of Satan to fight against themselves.

We pray that Christians would agree with each other, enter into spiritual warfare and expose evil to the world. We pray that Americans will put their hope in GOD, and for our government and victims of terrorism.

We pray that everyone will see that their lives are threatened by Islam that does not tolerate anyone who does not believe in Allah. Show the world that Allah is not GOD. Islamic teaching from the Koran of violence results in terrible deeds, brutal dehumanizing treatment of women, persecution and elimination of non-Muslims, millions killed, thousands enslaved, no freedom of religion and the press, crimes charged against Christians, and conversion from Islam to Christianity ends in death.

For The Persecuted
DEAR HEAVENLY AND GRACIOUS FATHER, we pray for those who suffer persecution, widows and orphans of martyrs, and families of those who are imprisoned, kidnapped, degraded, persecuted, ostracized, abandoned, tortured, murdered, mutilated, oppressed, poverty, malnutrition, conflict, chronic instability, slavery, debt bondage, serfdom; **forced child prostitution, soldiers, exploitation and labor;** pornography, making and selling drugs, genital mutilation, abortion, fatigue, **HIV, AIDS, sickness and disease,** confiscation, sex trade, refused basic education, competitive control, **girls valued less than boys,** prejudice, lust, hate, hopelessness, brutality, violence, witchcraft, curses, **abused sexually, physically, emotionally and violently,** and evil ancient traditions.

For Loved Ones
DEAR HEAVENLY AND GRACIOUS FATHER, we pray for our loved ones. We confess Your Word over **(your loved ones)** (Moody's and Hughes', Chauncey's and Wilson's, Levy's and Hendrey's, Hostetler's/Kalkans) this day. **Your Word will not return void to You and will accomplish what it says You will do. Thank You for this supernatural work.** Teach us HOLY SPIRIT how to pray.

We believe that JESUS CHRIST is the Great Conqueror of the devils of darkness. We bind the powers, principalities, rulers of wickedness in high places, and the demonic spirits of the air, earth and seas that are binding the life our loved ones and their families.

We command every evil spirit that has their wills bound and tell you to loose their wills. You will no longer bind their minds. We loose their minds to the Gospel of Grace. We bind your powers over their spirits, souls and bodies. We command the demons that are motivating and driving the sins of lust, drugs, alcohol, spiritual blindness and AntiChrist to cease their activities.

We bless You FATHER. We ask that you send warring angels over our loved ones and extend Your Grace to their salvation. We pray that You open their spiritual eyes and deafened ears to hear Your Word.

FATHER, we praise You and honor YOUR SON, JESUS CHRIST. We thank You for Your Love towards us even when we were in sin. **We thank You for Your Divine Deliverance.** We rejoice in their salvation and believe that You are moving on their behalf. Thank You FATHER that You are dispatching warring angels to war for their souls. Praise You for sending workers in the fields across their pathway. **We worship You FATHER.** Praise You that THE HOLY SPIRIT is bringing conviction to our loved ones of sin and revealing JESUS CHRIST'S SACRIFICE to them.

For Jews And Hebrews

We pray for Jews around the world to come into THE SAVING KNOWLEDGE OF JESUS CHRIST, Israel for its protection from enemies, messianic congregations, evangelistic organizations that are leading Jews to become Christians and Hebrews that have become Christians who sometimes call themselves Messianic Jews.

How And What

DEAR HEAVENLY AND GRACIOUS FATHER, we pray for our own particular needs: salvation of family members, finances, healing and other needs. For the needs of others and any prayer requests that have come in. For the work of local churches, **(your church)** and Chapel on the Campus. For prayer groups, world revival and for Israel. **For the peace of Jerusalem: May they prosper who love you** (Psa. 122:6).

That GOD's people will be ready for JESUS CHRIST'S SECOND COMING (II Cor. 11:2). For ministries training laborers for the harvest. JESUS CHRIST said, **Therefore pray THE LORD of the harvest to send out laborers into His harvest** (Matt. 9:38). **For kings, and for <u>all that are in authority</u>; that we may lead a quiet and peaceable life in <u>all Godliness and honesty</u>** (I Tim. 2:2) and the leaders of my country, that they will be providentially guided in their decisions.

WE ASK IN THE NAME OF JESUS CHRIST, LORD, MASTER AND SAVIOR

AGAINST TERRORISM

We come together in unity of THE HOLY SPIRIT with other Christians around the world against terrorism. We ask for the protection of THE BLOOD AND NAME OF THE LORD JESUS CHRIST. We pray according to The Holy Bible and Psalm 91 which is very powerful.

GENERAL
Praise, Honor And Worship

BLESSING, GLORY, WISDOM, THANKSGIVING, HONOR, POWER, AND MIGHT, BE UNTO OUR GOD FOR EVER AND EVER. WE PRAISE, EXALT AND WORSHIP THE FATHER, SON, HOLY SPIRIT. We thank You for Your Divine Deliverance And Supernatural Work. We thank You for Your Love Towards Us even when we were in sin. We believe that JESUS CHRIST is the Great Conqueror of the devils of darkness.

Praise You that THE HOLY SPIRIT is bringing conviction to our loved ones of sin, and revealing JESUS CHRIST'S SACRIFICE to them. THANK YOU FATHER that You are dispatching warring angels to war for their souls. Praise You for sending workers in the fields across their pathway. We rejoice in their salvation, and believe that You are moving on their behalf.

General

For: National Repentance, Revival, Those in Authority, Good Government, Sanctity of Life, Marriage, Family, Education, Church, Israel, End-Time Restoration, National Security, Supremacy of CHRIST, Racial Reconciliation, Religious Freedom, Widows, Orphans and Peace. Maintaining Christian orthodoxy; restoring biblical world view; public display and observance of The Ten Commandments; fulfillment of Great Commandment and Commission; preserving traditional marriage; thwarting same-sex marriage and adoption; and exposure of gangs, terrorists cells and networks, and THE COMPLETE WORD OF GOD.

Against: Abortion, Terrorism, Secular Humanism, New Age, Occult, Immigration, Poverty, HIV and AIDS, Slavery, Sex and Drug Trafficking, War, Alcoholism, Drug Addiction, Pornography, Sex Addiction, Child Abuse, Murder and Crime. Homelessness and hunger in America; economic downturn; national debt and corporate corruption; loss of U.S. sovereignty, and everything of The Kingdom Of Satan.

How To Pray

HOLY, HOLY, HOLY IS THE LORD GOD ALMIGHTY. Pray in The Fear of THE LORD. Battle evil forces of darkness. There is a void of prayer training in most seminaries.

We pray for the leaders of our country to be providentially guided in their decisions. Our needs: salvation of family members, finances, healing and other needs. Needs of others and prayer requests that have come in. Work of local churches (your church) and Chapel on the Campus. Ministries training laborers for the harvest. Prayer groups, world revival and Israel. GOD's people to be ready for JESUS CHRIST'S SECOND COMING (II Cor. 11:2).

Innocent blood has covered America and we surely deserve your judgement. Shake America and show our nation what you think about sins. Shake the churches and show Christians how they have failed America and You. We pray for everyone connected to this nation that they will turn from sin and come back to GOD. Show our churches how they are responsible for the spiritual state of the nation; Christians - the spiritual state of the world.

We pray that GOD will be THE LORD of America, expose evil to the world, unravel the interlocking of evil groups, bring confusion in their midst, defeat their plans and loose the heavenly powers against our enemies who want to destroy America. We command the powers of Satan to fight against themselves.

We pray that Christians would agree with each other, enter into spiritual warfare and expose evil to the world. We pray that Americans will put their hope in GOD, and for our government and victims of terrorism.

TACTICS
Agreement With Others
I am humbly grateful for those who have prayed for me, and I stand with them in prayer for their needs. I pray for Christians and those who do not know JESUS CHRIST AS LORD, MASTER AND SAVIOR.

Works Of God's Hands
Alexander the coppersmith did me much evil: THE LORD reward him according to his works (2 Tim. 4:14). THE LORD reward our enemies according to their works. We pray for deliverance and healing from the works of our enemies.

Hounds Of Heaven
FATHER, IN THE NAME OF JESUS CHRIST, BY THE POWER OF THE HOLY SPIRIT, we pray that you send The Hounds Of Heaven to sniff out, capture, bring back, recover and unveil what the enemy has stolen from us. We request that our property and missing persons be returned to us in good state and with no damage.

Lust For Money
We pray for those whose God Is Money and Worship Satan that are headed for Hell. We pray for their salvation and that GOD would cause them to see what they are doing to themselves. We pray that GOD will expose their actions to the world. We ask GOD for spiritual warfare against the forces of evil that control these people.

God Is Not Mocked - He Laughs!
I pray that you laugh at and mock your enemies, have them in derision and cause them to reap what they sow. We ask GOD to give us the heathen for our inheritance, and the uttermost parts of the earth for our possessions. We pray that the Godly bands will not be broken and the Godly cords cast away.

Covenant With God
We ask for personal relationships with GOD. We ask GOD to go before us and flow through us. We ask GOD to spiritually cleanse ourselves and what He has given us.

The Power Of The Blood

We cover us with THE BLOOD OF THE LAMB, JESUS CHRIST. We agree with THE COVENANT OF THE BLOOD. We sing songs about THE BLOOD OF JESUS CHRIST. We apply THE BLOOD, THE CROSS, THE COVENANT and THE WORD OF GOD which destroys death and power of the enemy.

We repent of any sin. With THE STRIPES OF JESUS CHRIST, we are healed (Isa. 53:4-5; 1 Pet. 2:24). THE BLOOD OF JESUS CHRIST was shed for our atonement and physical healing. THE LIFE OF JESUS CHRIST is driving out our sickness, disease and weakness. We pray, meditate and praise THE LORD JESUS CHRIST for salvation, healing and wholeness.

Guardian And Warrior Angels

We ask GOD to put a hedge around us, seal our property and possessions with angels, and send angels to be stationed on our properties to guard us. We call for THE ANGEL OF THE LORD to fight for us. We ask GOD to send guardian and warrior angels, and twelve legions of angels as reinforcement for spiritual and physical warfare on our behalf. We ask for warrior angels to protect us and fight for us. We ask the angels to remove the ropes, shackles, chains, bonds and bands from those being ministered to. See Psa. 34:7 & 91:11-13; Heb. 1:14.

We ask GOD to send angels ahead of us to prepare the way, for the angels to go with us wherever we go, and leave angels where we have ministered to continue the works. We ask the angels to read Scripture to the demons until they leave. We ask GOD to send His Anger, Wrath, Indignation And Trouble on those who would destroy Christianity. We ask GOD to send angels with boxes to separately seal each demon in, chain and gag the demons, read Scripture to the demons and fill the boxes with THE GLORY OF GOD.

Doorways

Forgive us for defiling THE TEMPLE OF GOD, and demonic imaginations and visualizations (witchcraft). We confess sins and iniquities (sins, wickedness and evil deeds) of our fathers and nation. We forgive those who have sinfully affected us. We ask GOD to close demonic doorways. We ask GOD to cleanse by THE POWER AND BLOOD OF JESUS CHRIST.

Psalms: God's Pronouncements

We forgive the Catholic Church, and other religions, organizations and people for cursing Christians with anath'e'ma. We break and reverse the great curses, damnation and destruction placed on us and our descendants.

Psalm 109

Hold not thy peace, O GOD my praise: For the mouth of the wicked and the mouth of the deceitful are opened against me: they have spoken against me with a lying tongue. They compassed me about also with words of hatred; and fought against me without a cause. For my love they are my adversaries: but I give myself unto prayer. And they have rewarded me evil for good, and hatred for my love.

Territorial Warfare

WE ASK GOD FOR THE HEATHEN FOR OUR INHERITANCE, AND THE UTTERMOST PARTS OF THE EARTH FOR OUR POSSESSION. WE ASK AND RECEIVE; SEEK AND FIND; KNOCK AND IT WILL BE OPENED. We stand in the gap. We ask GOD for families, ministries, churches, parishes, counties, cities, states, nations and the world that The Gospel would be proclaimed and bear fruit. We ask GOD to restrain the territorial darkness that would prevent The Gospel. We ask GOD to persecute them for their ungodly acts.

Tactics To Win The War Against Satan

Forgive us for: failure to align ourselves with GOD's WILL, known sin and rebellion, emotional stress and trauma, submissions to an ungodly cover, inherited curses, worldly art and music, ownership of unclean objects; failure to cleanse property and places, and tithe; unforgiveness, idolatry, and a lack of separation from the things of the world. We agree to cleanse our beings, possessions and homes of unclean objects. We ask for forgiveness, confess contact with the occult and sins of the fathers, and renounce evil.

We ask for: THE FRUITS, GIFTS, SIGNS, ANOINTING and LEADERSHIP OF THE HOLY SPIRIT, THE AUTHORITY OF JESUS CHRIST and THE POWER OF ALMIGHTY GOD to minister to the people. We stand behind the protection: THE HEDGE OF GOD (Job 1 & 2) and our shield of faith (Eph. 6:16).

Returning Curses

We forgive, repent and renounce involvement in Inheritance, Unclean and Unholy Things, Territorial Rights Violations, Performance Of Demonic Rituals, Distinct Situations And Actions, and General. We forgive and repent for our nationalities, ancestors, ourselves, descendents, mates and others for cursing us. We break the curses placed on us from these sources.

I pray that GOD will destroy the weapons of His enemies. I pray that GOD will use His Weapons against our enemies.

CHRISTIANITY
For Christianity

We pray for GOD's Good and against Satan's Evil. We pray for Jehovah's Religion and against Lucifer's False Religion. We pray for Christianity and against The New World Order which is AntiChrist. We pray for the coming of JESUS CHRIST, The True Messiah, and against Satan, The False Messiah.

For Apostate Church

We pray for the Apostate Church that you would awake them and show them THE JUDGEMENT OF GOD. We pray that you would bring deliverance into The Church. We pray for signs, wonders and miracles brought by THE POWER AND ANOINTING OF GOD. We pray for Christians everywhere to enter into spiritual warfare.

13

We bind fallen angels and demons, and loose ourselves from them. We call for spiritual warfare to set the captives free. We bind forces of evil, and loose forces of good that we have the power and authority to do so.

AGAINST VIOLENT WEATHER

Violent Weather: We fast, pray and have faith in GOD. We have the right to use THE NAME OF JESUS CHRIST because we are Christians. This gives us the authority to command the weather caused by evil forces. We bind satanic power of evil weather. We loose THE POWER OF GOD to bring restoration from violent weather.

We bind and take authority over territorial spirits in the second heaven ruling over demonic weather and hurricanes. We ask the warring angels to destroy the winds, waves and violent weather.

We ask for supernatural protection of GOD's people, that there would be no injuries or deaths, nor any damage to their homes or property. We pray for protection of Christians as judgement comes upon America and the world.

Hurricanes: We pray a shield of JESUS between the water and the winds, so the spirits of Poseidon, Leviathan, Neptune and Hercules can not rise up out of the waters, and give strength and acceleration to the spirits of storms, hurricanes, tornadoes, high winds, destructive winds and killer winds. We dispatch Michael and the warring angels into the storm and capture all of the demon spirits to destroy the storm.

We bind the God of the hurricane (name of hurricane). We speak confusion into the mind of the hurricane. We command the hurricane to weaken. We reverse the curses of witchcraft affecting violent weather.

AGAINST WITCHCRAFT

My son pray My Word, Ex. 22:18, Thou shalt not suffer a witch to live. Gen. 6:3a And THE LORD said, My Spirit shall not always strive with man. We release Your Word to do its work according to Your Will and as You direct by YOUR SPIRIT.

FOR NATIONAL SINS

We forgive America FOR THE SINS COMMITTED ESPECIALLY THE SHEDDING OF INNOCENT BLOOD, AND AGREEMENT AND FINANCIAL ASSISTANCE TO OTHER NATIONS TO SHED INNOCENT BLOOD. We are cursed by sins of America. We break national curses and that have come upon us and our descendents.

FOR JUDGMENTS

We ask that You shake and awake The World, America and Christianity before Satan takes over in The Tribulation. ALMIGHTY GOD, nothing happens without your permission because You are in complete control. We ask that Christians pray to GOD and enter into spiritual warfare daily against Satan's Kingdom Of Evil. We agree with THE JUDGMENTS OF GOD and ask that You have mercy on Christians.

We ask that you bring judgement on The World, America and THE CHURCH OF JESUS CHRIST so that they will repent of their sins. The four sore acts of judgement include the sword, famine, pestilence and noisome beasts (war, starvation, disease and ferocious animals). We ask that You have mercy and grace on true Christians (the elect and remnant) in the midst of judgement. ALMIGHTY GOD, we deserve and accept Your Judgement which is perfect.

Pray specifically for what you are facing. Satan, God Of This World, can only do what You allow him to do. We ask that You send warring angels, ministering angels, THE HOLY SPIRIT AND THE SEVEN FOLD SPIRIT OF GOD to do battle with supernatural troubles, calamities and disasters not of GOD.

FOR PERSECUTED CHURCH

We pray for persecuted and martyred Christian brothers and sisters around the world, The Persecuted Church, those who pray for The Persecuted Church, agencies that support the Persecuted Church and those who persecute The Church. We pray for Islam, Hinduism, Buddhism, Chinese, Animism, Atheism, tribal religions, and non-Christian religions that persecute Christians. We pray for THE BODY OF CHRIST as we suffer more persecution. We pray for strength in persecution so that we will not deny JESUS CHRIST.

We pray for those who suffer persecution, widows and orphans of martyred, and families of those who are: intimidated, raped, harassed, tortured, pressured to renounce their faith, discriminated against; denied health care, education and jobs; starved, murdered, hearts broken, stripped of human dignity, poor, refugees and marginalized, imprisoned, kidnapped, degraded, ostracized, abandoned, mutilated, oppressed, malnutrition, conflict, chronic instability, slavery, debt bondage, serfdom; forced child prostitution, soldiers, exploitation and labor; pornography, making and selling drugs, genital mutilation, abortion, fatigue, HIV, AIDS, sickness and disease, confiscation, sex trade, competitive control, girls valued less than boys, prejudice, lust, hate, hopelessness, brutality, violence, witchcraft, curses; abused sexually, physically, emotionally and violently, and evil ancient traditions.

We pray for everyone associated with: American Civil Liberties Union, Freedom From Religious Foundation, National Organization For Women, Americans United For Separation Of church And State, Planned Parenthood, People For The American Way, NARAL, Pro-choice America, National Abortion Federation, Feminist Majority Foundation, and their allies to come into THE SAVING KNOWLEDGE OF JESUS CHRIST.

SECTION 3 - CURSES DELIVERANCE PRAYERS

WE ASK IN THE NAME OF JESUS CHRIST, LORD, MASTER AND SAVIOR.

CONTENTS

WORD CURSES
Christian Fantasy

I forgive those who have controlled me with charismatic witchcraft. Please forgive me for practicing witchcraft and trying to control other people's wills. I take authority over these evil forces, break evil soul ties and break curses placed on me.

Lies, Deceit And Flattery

Father, I want to be like you; you do not lie. I want The Truth to be in me. I repent for being a liar, a deceitful person, being a cheat and dishonest, flattering other people, giving a false appearance, having pride, ego and vanity, being false and faithless, pretending I am something other than what I am, and for falseness of dress, thoughts and actions. Help me to be what you made me to be; I want to be natural and not false.

BIBLICAL CURSES

I forgive my ancestors and anyone else that has cursed me. I break curses placed on me or my descendants from uttering a wish of evil against one; to imprecate evil, to call for mischief or injury to fall upon; to execrate, to bring evil upon or to; to blast, vex, harass or torment with great calamities. I break these curses. I break the curses back to ten generations or even to Adam and Eve on both sides of my family, and destroy legal holds and legal grounds that demons have to work in my life.

I now rebuke, break, loose myself and my children from evil curses, charms, vexes, hexes, spells, jinxes, psychic powers, bewitchment, witchcraft and sorcery, that have been put

16

upon me or my family line from persons or from occult or psychic sources, and I cancel connected or related spirits and command them to leave me. I thank you for setting me free.

AMERICAN INDIAN CURSES

I forgive American Indians and my Indian ancestors for witchcraft against the white man, me and my relatives; for deep-hidden-seething anger-bitterness-resentment-hatred of the white man; for cursing the land and people; for eating and drinking flesh and blood; and for worshipping demons. I forgive the white man for rejecting and enslaving them on the reservation. I forgive the war women for the Jezebelic matriarchal rule of the tribe.

I forgive the witch doctors and shamans for cursing the descendents, dedicating them to Satan, and causing physical problems and diseases. I forgive my ancestors.

I ask forgiveness for myself for the sin of idol worship and disobedience as described in Exodus 20, Leviticus 26 and Ezekiel 18. I ask you to forgive me for sins associated with Indians such as Scouting. I will destroy Indian artifacts, break ungodly soul ties and break ties to Indian organizations.

I break the curses of incest, rape, immorality and the bastard. I break spiritual roots to diseases brought about by curses. I break American Indian curses on me and my descendents back to when the white man came to America.

I come against spirits that have been renounced and legal rights taken away.

ALASKAN NATIVE CURSES
Prayer

I forgive my ancestors, descendents and others, ask you to forgive me and I forgive myself for worshiping traditions and idols, alcohol and drug abuse, rape, sexual abuse and perversion, murder, self bitterness and hatred, occult, Americans and religions for suppressing religious and cultural practices, having to depend on welfare, reversing gender roles; multiple spouses; false religions and demonic beliefs, ceremonies, dances and rituals, having demonic paraphernalia,

talismans, amulets, charms, spirit poles, objects, adornment and tattoos; sins of Alaskan Natives, Indians and Eskimos; Russians, traders, soldiers and others for mistreating my ancestors; those who brought alcoholism, drug addiction, heart disease, diabetes, fetal alcohol syndrome, serious abuse of women and children, incarceration and suicide upon my people; being warlike, taking slaves, barbarism, torture and cruelty; following shamans and wise men;

for worshiping and following demons; tribes, clans and groups for their demonic beliefs; preferential female infanticide; following myths and legends; transvestites, adultery, wife swapping and incest; seeking help from evil spirits; worshipping animals and their spirits; reincarnation and ancestor worship; acquiring guardian spirits; seeking forbidden knowledge; demonic healing and divination; worship of nature and earth;

17

transformation into animals and animals into humans; fears of death and shamans; mistreating and killing slaves; cutting the flesh; using human fat and mummies; magic and witchcraft; superstition and taboos; insanity, severe sickness, early death and diseases of Alaska. We come against spirits that have been renounced and legal rights taken away, and command that they come out with their families and works as their names are called.

To Break Curses

I forgive my ancestors and descendents; I ask You to forgive me and I forgive myself for sins which bring these curses on me. I break the following curses. exotic and old diseases, and new viruses, AIDS, ebola and ecoli; killer bees, ants, locusts and flies bringing devastation and disease; sin, trespass, disobedience and iniquity; cover up, act secretly and treacherously; moral, social, spiritual and land hardships; reverse prejudice, racism, division,

rebellion and loneliness; prehistoric terrorism; pain, terror and defilement; attacks of earthly leaders and demonic powers; anger, frustration, resentment, bitterness, revenge and pride; disease, domestic violence, hatred and broken relationships; child, spouse, drug and alcohol, and financial and substance abuse; hallucinogenic drug in peyote.

AFRICAN AMERICAN CURSES
Breaking The Willie Lynch Curse

I forgive Willie Lynch and those involved in slave trade and slave use throughout time whether in the Black or White Race. I forgive those who treat the Black Race as slaves today. I forgive those who want to lynch me personally, ministerially and business-wise today. I pray that you would forgive and bless them with spiritual blessings, especially salvation.

I break the curse of Willie Lynch off of me and my bloodline going back to 1712 and earlier. I now break curses placed on me by those involved in slavery and those who treat me like a slave. I command the demons restore to me and my family what they have stolen from us.

Walls Of Argument

I forgive black men, black women and black youth for the way they have treated me. Forgive me for the way I have treated them.

CURSING OTHERS AND BEING CURSED

Father, we want to bless others and be blessed rather than to curse others and be cursed. Please make us a blessing and take away the curse. We will get rid of cursed objects in our possession. We ask that you, other people and our descendents forgive us for anything we have done to bring the curse. We forgive our ancestors and others that have placed curses on us. Please forgive these people for psychic prayers, spoken curses, ancestral curses, parental curses, cursing by others, cursing ourselves, cursing our descendents, disobedience, Ahab and Jezebel, charismatic witchcraft, conceiving bastards, having incest, Indian curses, and other curse known or unknown that is found in THE HOLY WORD OF GOD.

I now break curses placed on me or my descendants. I break the curses back to ten generations or even to Adam and Eve on both sides of my family, and destroy legal holds and legal grounds that demons have to work in my life. I break curses that follow:

CURSES FOR SHEDDING INNOCENT BLOOD

Dear Father in Heaven, there are curses that fall on individuals, families, races and nations for the sin of shedding innocent blood. This is a curse that travels down the family line. I ask for forgiveness for myself and those before me who have sinned against you and others by shedding innocent blood.

We have greatly erred in shedding innocent blood in the United States. Forgive us of this terrible sin, redeem us from quilt and cleanse the land.

I repent of having become involved in acts that show worship and obedience to the Devil and his demons. I repent of occult acts: worship, drugs, sex, thievery, murder, etc. I break soul ties with others that I practiced these acts with.

You have given us power over the power of the Devil. I break the curse of shedding innocent blood off my family and my descendents. I break curses of idol worship, Satanism and illicit sex.

You have said that if I call on You, I can be delivered. I thank you for what you have done for me. I commit my life to you in a greater way than I have before. Please instruct me, help me to correct my life and bring it into subjection to You.

HOUSE CURSES
Cleaning Your House

I come to you about cursed objects and demon infestation in my possessions and home, and in me. I forgive my ancestors, descendants and others who have had spiritual influence over me. I ask you to forgive and bless them, especially with salvation. Please forgive me and I forgive myself for spiritual adultery. I forgive those who have cursed me; forgive me for cursing others. I break the curses and demonic soul ties including psychic and Catholic prayers. I will clean out my house of cursed objects or exorcise objects that I don't own. I will anoint my house with oil and drive the evil spirits out of the house. Show me cursed objects, demon infestation and spirits that need to be cast out of people.

CURSE OF PRIDE

I come to you in the matter of pride. Pride is an abomination to you. I renounce pride and turn away from it. I humble myself before you and come to you as a little child. I ask you to forgive me and I forgive myself. I do this for sins committed in pride that would have affected me.

I forgive my ancestors, descendents, and anyone else that has had spiritual or carnal authority over me. I ask that you save them, bless them with spiritual blessings, bring them into truth and meet their needs out of your riches in glory.

CURSE OF AHAB AND JEZEBEL

I ask you to forgive me and I forgive my ancestors for being Jezebels and Ahabs. Please forgive me for idol worship, passivity, irresponsibility, fear, weakness, sexual impurity, pride, selfishness, witchcraft, control, criticism, jealousy, rebellion, competition, retaliation, marriage breaking, child abuse and worshiping other Gods.

WE ASK IN THE NAME OF JESUS CHRIST, LORD, MASTER AND SAVIOR.

CONTENTS

DELIVERANCE WARFARE
Short
LORD JESUS CHRIST, I believe you died on the cross for my sins and rose again from the dead. You redeemed me by your blood and I belong to you, and I want to live for you. I confess my sins, known and unknown, I'm sorry for them. I renounce them. I forgive

others as I want you to forgive me. (Pause to allow forgiveness of others as THE HOLY SPIRIT leads.)

Forgive me and cleanse me with your blood. I thank you for THE BLOOD OF JESUS CHRIST which cleanses me from sin. I come to you as my deliverer. You know my special needs: the thing that binds, that torments, that defiles, that evil spirit, that unclean spirit. I claim the promise of your word, Whosoever that calleth on THE NAME OF THE LORD shall be delivered. I call upon you; deliver me and set me free. Satan, I renounce you and your works. I loose myself from you.

Medium

LORD JESUS CHRIST, thank you for dying for my sins, for your glorious resurrection and for making me a new creature in CHRIST by faith in your precious blood. I have sought supernatural experience apart from you and disobeyed your Word.

I want you to help me renounce these things and cleanse me in body, soul and spirit. I renounce witchcraft and magic, both black and white; Ouija boards and occult games; seances, clairvoyance and mediums; ESP, second sight, and mind reading; fortune telling, palm reading, tea-leaf reading, crystal balls, Tarot and card laying; astrology and interest in horoscopes; the heresy of reincarnation and healing groups involved in metaphysics; hypnosis;

curiosity about future or past, and which is outside Thy Will; water witching and dowsing, levitation, body lifting, table tipping, psychometry and automatic writing; astral projection and demonic skills; literature I read in these fields and vow that I will destroy such books in my own possession; psychic and occult; cults that deny THE BLOOD OF CHRIST; philosophies that deny THE DIVINITY OF CHRIST; and evil spirits that bind and torment me.

I break curses placed on me from occult sources; psychic heredity, and demonic holds upon my family line as a result of the disobedience of my ancestors; bonds of physical and mental illness; and demonic subjection to my mother, father, grandparents and human beings. I call upon THE LORD JESUS CHRIST to set me free.

Long
Forgiveness

ALMIGHTY GOD, I have a confession to make: I have not loved, but have resented certain people and have unforgiveness in my heart, and I call upon you to help me forgive them. I do forgive (name them, both living and dead) and ask you to forgive them. I do forgive and accept myself.

General Confession

LORD JESUS CHRIST, I believe that you are THE SON OF GOD, that you are the Messiah come in the flesh to destroy the works of the Devil. You died on the cross for my sins and rose again from the dead. I renounce unbelief and doubt as sin. I confess my sins and repent. I ask you to forgive me. I believe that your blood cleanses me from sin.

Pride, Ego And Vanity

ALMIGHTY GOD, I come to you. These six things doth THE LORD hate: yea, seven are an abomination unto him: a proud look, a lying tongue, hands that shed innocent blood, a heart that deviseth wicked imaginations, feet that be swift in running to mischief, a false witness that speaketh lies, and he that soweth discord among brethren. I renounce these and turn away from them. I humble myself before you and come to you as a little child.

Come To JESUS, THE DELIVERER

ALMIGHTY GOD, I come to you as my Deliverer. You know my problems (name them), the things that bind, that torment, that defile and harass me. I loose myself from evil spirits and influences, and satanic bondages.

Prince's BLOOD OF JESUS

Through the Blood of THE LORD JESUS CHRIST, I am redeemed out of the hand of the Devil. My sins are forgiven. I am justified, made righteous, just as if I'd never sinned. I am made holy, set apart to GOD. My body is a temple for THE HOLY SPIRIT, redeemed, cleansed, sanctified. THE BLOOD OF JESUS CHRIST cleanses me from sin. Satan has no part in me, no power over me. I renounce Satan, loose myself from him, command him to leave me, in THE NAME OF THE LORD JESUS CHRIST!

Church's Command

In THE NAME OF THE LORD JESUS CHRIST, I command Satan and his demons to loose my mind. I ask you to send angels to break, cut and sever fetters, bands, ties and bonds, whether they be by word or deed. I ask you to loose THE SEVEN-FOLD SPIRIT OF GOD: SPIRIT OF THE LORD, FEAR OF THE LORD, COUNSEL, MIGHT, WISDOM, KNOWLEDGE, AND UNDERSTANDING into me and my family.

Restoring The Soul

You can insert the names of the person / persons that you are praying for, rather than your name in the prayer.

ALMIGHTY GOD, I ask you to send angels to gather and restore my soul to its rightful place in me. I ask for you to send your angels to unearth and break earthen vessels, bonds, bands and bindings that have been put upon my soul, willingly or unawares. I ask you to have them free my soul from bondage by whatever means is required. THE LORD JESUS CHRIST is powerful and effective to do this.

I ask you to send your angels to gather and restore the pieces of my fragmented mind, will and emotions to their proper place. Bring them into their original positions perfectly as you planned them when you formed Adam and Eve in the Garden of Eden.

I have power and authority that has been delegated to me. I break, cast out and return to the sender, the power of curses upon my head and soul.

Warfare

ALMIGHTY GOD, I bow in worship and praise before you. I cover myself with the Blood of THE LORD JESUS CHRIST as my protection. I surrender myself completely and unreservedly in areas of my life to you. I take a stand against the workings of Satan that would hinder me in my prayer life. I address myself only to the true and living GOD, and refuse involvement of Satan in my prayer. Satan, I command you to leave my presence with your demons. I bring the Blood of THE LORD JESUS CHRIST between us. I resist the endeavors of Satan and his wicked spirits to rob me of the will of GOD. I choose to be transformed by the renewing of my mind. I pull down the strongholds of Satan.

MOODYS'
Sins Of Ancestors, Curses, Soul Ties, Fragmented Soul And Subconscious Mind

I forgive my ancestors (upwards), descendants (downwards), and others (outwards) that have sinned against GOD and hurt me (those outside of me). I ask you to forgive them for their sins and mistakes. I remit their sins, sever demonic ties, and set myself free. I ask GOD to bless them with spiritual blessings, bring them into truth, and meet their needs out of His Riches in Glory through CHRIST JESUS. I ask that GOD forgive me (Godwards) for my sins, and I forgive myself (inwards) for sins against my body.

I ask You to send the gifts of THE HOLY SPIRIT to minister to the needs of the people and accomplish what you want done. I am careful to give you the glory, honor, praise and credit for what is said and done. These things I ask in the blessed NAME OF JESUS CHRIST: LORD, MASTER AND SAVIOR.

I command the forces of evil to obey in THE NAME OF JESUS CHRIST. I take authority over Satan and the forces of evil according to the HOLY BIBLE, the complete WORD OF GOD, and command that you obey it. I break curses, charms, spells, jinxes, psychic powers, hexes, vexes and demonic ties that bind. I break soul ties caused by witchcraft, sorcery, bewitchment and sexual sins. Restore my fragmented soul: mind, will and emotions; send your angels out to recover what Satan has stolen from me. Stir up the demons in my subconscious mind so that they can be identified and cast out.

Taking Spiritual Authority Over The Meeting

Behold, I give unto you power to tread on serpents and scorpions (big and little demons), and over all the power of the enemy, and nothing shall by any means hurt you (Luke 10:19). We come against powers, principalities, evil forces in this world and spiritual wickedness in high places. We come against demons inside or outside of anyone present, over this city, state, nation and world, in Hell or out of Hell. We come against you by THE POWER AND BLOOD OF JESUS CHRIST, by THE WORD OF GOD, by THE NAME OF JESUS,

by the authority of the believer, in the unity of our spirits, to set ourselves free. We sit in heavenly places over Satan, fallen angels, demons and forces of evil. We command you to line up in rank, file and order, and come out quickly. We bind the power that you have and loose ourselves from you in THE NAME OF JESUS CHRIST of Nazareth. We take authority over Satan and the kingdom of evil according to THE WHOLE WORD OF GOD. Amen!

DELIVERANCE WARFARE WITH LISTS
Biblical Curses

ALMIGHTY GOD, I forgive my ancestors and others that have cursed me. I ask that GOD forgive me and them. I break curses placed on me and my descendants from uttering a wish of evil against one; to imprecate evil, to call for mischief and injury to fall upon; to execrate, to bring evil upon and to; to blast, vex, harass and torment with great calamities. I break the curses back to ten generations and even to Adam and Eve on both sides of my family, and destroy legal holds and grounds that demons have to work in my life.

I rebuke, break, loose myself and my children from evil curses, charms, vexes, hexes, spells, jinxes, psychic powers, bewitchment, witchcraft and sorcery that have been put upon me and my family line from persons, occult and psychic sources, and I cancel connected and related spirits and command them to leave me. I thank you, LORD, for setting me free. But it shall come to pass, if thou wilt not hearken unto the voice of THE LORD THY GOD, to observe to do all His commandments and His statutes which I command thee this day; that all these curses shall come upon thee, and overtake thee. I break these curses and those that follow in THE NAME OF THE LORD JESUS CHRIST.

Soul Ties

ALMIGHTY GOD, I break and renounce evil soul ties with engagements, lodges, adulterers, close friends, husbands, wives, cults and binding agreements between buddies.

Forgive me for developing evil soul ties. I forgive those who would control me. I renounce these evil soul ties, break them and wash them away with the shed blood of THE LORD JESUS CHRIST.

Occult And False Religion

ALMIGHTY GOD, I confess seeking from Satan the help that should only come from You. I confess occultism and false religions as sin. I repent and renounce these sins and ask you to forgive me. I renounce Satan and his works: I hate his demons; I count them my enemies. I close the door on occult practices, and I command such spirits to leave me.

I renounce, break and loose myself and my children from psychic powers, bondages, and bonds of physical and mental illness, upon me and my family line, as the results of parents and other ancestors.

I renounce, break and loose myself from demonic subjection to my mother, father, grandparents, and other human beings, living and dead, that have dominated me.

I forgive my ancestors and ask that you would forgive me for participating in occult and false religion. I renounce fortune telling, magic practices and spiritism, cults and false teachings, and Satan worship. I break curses and soul ties brought about by psychic heredity, occult contacts and religious cults. I break demonic holds on my family line due to supernatural experiences apart from GOD.

Ungodly Spirits
ALMIGHTY GOD, I forgive my ancestors and ask that you forgive me for the following families of ungodly spirits and command that they come out as their name is called.

Godly Spirits
ALMIGHTY GOD, we ask that you direct the angels to minister to our needs. We loose warring angels, ministering angels, THE HOLY SPIRIT and THE SEVEN-FOLD SPIRIT OF GOD. We loose legions of angels including Godly spirits.

Cursed Objects And Demon Infestation
ALMIGHTY GOD, I ask that you forgive me for having cursed objects in my home. Show me by THE HOLY SPIRIT what to destroy.

SPECIAL
ALMIGHTY GOD, please forgive me for practicing mind control over anyone or having anything to do with programming the total mind control slave. I forgive those who have practiced mind control over me in anyway.

BASIC DELIVERANCE
ALMIGHTY GOD, I forgive those who have rejected me, been bitter against me and have rebelled against me. Please forgive me for rejection, bitterness and rebellion against others.

In THE NAME OF JESUS CHRIST I command the spirits to come out of the Unconscious, Subconscious and Conscious Mind. I command the families of Rejection, Bitterness and Rebellion, and other families to come out of me and bring their works with them.

ABUSED CHILDREN
ALMIGHTY GOD, please forgive me for abusing others mentally, physically, spiritually, materially and sexually. I forgive everyone that has abused me in those ways. I command every spirit of abuse, victimization and related spirits to come out of me in THE NAME OF JESUS CHRIST.

GRIEF AND BITTERNESS
ALMIGHTY GOD, please forgive me for the bitterness that I have from the grief over the loss of my loved ones and from any situation that has happened in my life. I repent for allowing natural grief to turn into demonic grief. I break demonic soul ties with the living and dead. I set myself free from demonic ties that came in through grief and bitterness. I command the families of grief and bitterness, and any related spirits to leave me in THE NAME OF JESUS CHRIST.

BASTARDS AND INCEST

ALMIGHTY GOD, I forgive my ancestors for creating bastards and committing incest. Please forgive me for the same sins. I break the curses of the bastard and incest on me and my descendents. I command the following spirits of sexual sins and diseases to come out of me in THE NAME OF JESUS CHRIST. (Use the OVERALL LIST OF DEMONS for sex.)

CHARISMATIC WITCHCRAFT

ALMIGHTY GOD, please forgive me for practicing charismatic witchcraft. I break the power of the ruler demons over my family and organization. I break demonic ties, bonds and caps. I break soul ties to pastors, religious leaders and any Christian who has been trying to control me. I break curses placed on me by submitting my will to others. I break curses brought by charismatic witchcraft and control. I break the curse of Jezebel and Ahab. I renounce false gifts given by Satan. I drive out demonic works and associated spirits of witchcraft and mind control in THE NAME OF JESUS CHRIST.

DRUNKENNESS AND GLUTTONY

ALMIGHTY GOD, I Forgive those who have rejected me and caused me to seek food and drink for comfort. I ask GOD for forgiveness for drunkenness and gluttony, and any other addictions such as drugs and medicines. I forgive my ancestors who were drunkards and gluttons, and break curses and demonic ties on me.

PERFECT LOVE

ALMIGHTY GOD, I thank You that You loved me so much that You died on the Cross for me. Please forgive me for not loving you, my relatives and others. I forgive my relatives and others for not loving me. I command the families of inability to give and receive love, and any related spirits to leave me in THE NAME OF JESUS CHRIST.

INGRATITUDE

ALMIGHTY GOD, I repent for having ingratitude towards GOD and others. Please forgive me and help me to have an attitude of gratitude irregardless of what happens in my life. Let me have joy in THE LORD and rejoice in THE LORD always.

SELF

ALMIGHTY GOD, please forgive me for thinking more about myself than about You and others that You want me to love. I repent for miserable thoughts about myself. I will rejoice and have joy in You at all times and under all situations. I will love THE LORD MY GOD with all my heart, and with all my soul, and with all my mind. I will love my neighbor as myself. I will love my enemies. I command the family of self demons to come out of me in THE NAME OF JESUS CHRIST.

HOW NOT TO DO DELIVERANCE

ALMIGHTY GOD, please forgive me for agreeing with the doctrines of demons and not with the truth of THE HOLY SPIRIT, rejecting deliverance and rebelling against THE WORD OF GOD; having fears of deliverance, demons and people; and becoming bitter against GOD and man for me being in bondage.

SECTION 5 - SEXUAL DELIVERANCE PRAYERS

WE ASK IN THE NAME OF JESUS CHRIST, LORD, MASTER AND SAVIOR.

CONTENTS

BASIC DELIVERANCE

I forgive those who have rejected me, and been bitter and rebelled against me. Please forgive me for rejection, bitterness and rebellion against others and God. I command the families of Rejection, Bitterness and Rebellion to come out.

MAIN LIST

I confess my sexual sins and ask you to place them under Your Blood. I renounce them and am truly sorry for participation. I repent and ask forgiveness. I ask you to cleanse, heal and deliver me. JESUS became a curse for me on the Cross and blotted out the Handwriting Of Ordinances against me. I ask that The Holy Spirit reveal other sexual offenses in my life that I or my ancestors have committed.

I confess relationships with their activities, thoughts, desires and attitudes as sin: preoccupation with sensual desires, appetites and indulgences; longing and ardent desire for what is forbidden; inordinate affection, and unnatural and unrestrained passions and lusts; promoting or partaking of that which produces lewd emotions, and fosters sexual sin and lust; filthy communication: obscene and filthy language, conversation and jokes; lewd and obscene music, poetry, literature and art; pornography; acts of sodomy, adultery, immorality,

fornication, masturbation, oral sex, effeminacy and homosexuality; affection for and attachment to philosophies, religions, and life styles which glorify, promote and condone sexual conduct in thought, word and deed contrary to the standard of the Bible; sexual occult involvement, both known and unknown, by me or my ancestors; expression of these philosophies, religions and life styles in art, literature, mass media, and public practices and attitudes.

I thank you for forgiving and cleansing me from unrighteousness. I give my affections and life to You. I ask You to empower areas of my life, so they will be used in service to You. I renounce demonic ties of affection and ask that You help me with agape love.

I break demonic power and authority over my life and affections. I break the hold these sins have had on me. I break soul ties. I break inherited curses and those I have brought upon myself and my descendents. I break curses which have come to me as a result of demonic associations.

I remove myself from demonic authority exercised over me. I come against the demonic authorities who controlled and motivated my relationships. I reclaim ground that I have given to Satan in body, soul and spirit. The Book of Joel states that those who call on THE NAME OF THE LORD shall be delivered. I hate Satan, his demons and his works; I count that which offends You as my enemy. I accept your forgiveness and cleansing.

I have confessed my sins, and broken soul ties and curses, and I rebuke Satan. I am reclaiming every area of my soul and body which I formerly gave to Satan. I claim freedom and cleansing in the areas of sexual sin. I renounce Satan and his hosts, and command that they leave me now. I take authority over every demon who has inhabited my mind, will and emotions, and body because of ungodly friendships.

I ask for your cleansing power. I forgive ancestors who have cursed me by their sexual sins. I ask that my descendents forgive me for the curses I have placed on them. I ask you to forgive me for not protecting those you entrusted to my care. I break soul ties with men or women that I have had sexual relations with. I ask that you sever these ties. I forgive those who have hurt me. I ask you to forgive me for having unforgiveness in my heart for others. I ask you to send health and healing to my body and soul. Please restore my family and me. I am thankful you have provided a way for me to be forgiven. I turn from my sins and follow you.

I command the families of demonic soul ties, fragmented soul, sexual lust, selfishness, sex with demons, pornography, sexual sins, and sexually transmitted diseases, dysfunctions and injuries to leave me.

ABNORMAL BEHAVIOR
Please forgive me for being a sexual partner with AIDS. I forgive anyone that would have infected me with AIDS in the following categories: anyone who has ever injected narcotics or non-prescribed drugs; any male who has ever had sex with another male; anyone who has ever engaged in sex for money or drugs; and anyone who has had sexual contact with a prostitute. I command the families of abnormal sexual behavior to come out.

ABORTION AND SHEDDING INNOCENT BLOOD

I ask for forgiveness for myself and those before me who have sinned against you and others by shedding innocent blood. We have greatly erred in shedding innocent blood, LORD forgive us this terrible sin and redeem us from quilt and cleanse the land.

We repent of having become involved in acts that show worship and obedience to the Devil and his demons. We repent of all occult acts: worship, drugs, sex, thievery, murder, etc. We break all soul ties with others that we practiced these acts with.

Because you have given us power over all the power of the Devil, I break this curse of shedding innocent blood off of my family and my descendents. I also break curses of idol worship, Satanism, illicit sex.

You have said that if I call on You I can be delivered. I thank You for all you have done for me. I commit my life to You in a greater way today than I have before. Please instruct me and help me to correct my life and bring it into subjection to You. Please forgive us for abortion, murder, killing and shedding innocent blood and being in agreement with these evil deeds. I command the families of abortion and shedding innocent blood to come out.

ABUSED CHILD

I forgive my ancestors, descendents and others; I ask you to forgive me and I forgive myself for sins of child abuse. I break inheritance from ancestors' sins that would give demons the right to be in the subconscious mind which include idol worship (Masons, occult, cults, Catholic, etc.), sexual sins (bastards, incest, adultery, homosexuality, etc.) and ungodly attitudes of the parents. I break Biblical curses relating to sexual impurity and ungodly soul ties with any person I have had sex with including animals. I break ties with Spirits of Abuse (demon spirits that went in from the abuser) and Victim Spirit (spirit that advertises to be victimized). I command the families of spirit of abuse, victim spirit and abused children spirits to come out.

DOMESTIC VIOLENCE

Please forgive me for any domestic violence that I have practiced against others. I am sorry and I repent for my sins.

I forgive those who have sinned and practiced domestic violence against me and my family. I forgive my ancestors or descendents, husbands or wives, boyfriends or girlfriends, and everyone that has had spiritual authority or any other type of control over me.

I forgive them for mental, physical, spiritual and material including emotional, sexual and any other type of abuse. I forgive them for controlling, battering, threatening and any ungodly action. I forgive them for threatening to commit suicide and to murder me.

May GOD bless them with spiritual blessings, bring them into truth and meet their needs out of his riches in glory through CHRIST JESUS. I pray especially for their salvation.

I now break any ungodly curses, soul ties and demonic holds that I have the authority and legal right before GOD to do so. I command the family of domestic violence spirits to come out.

EFFEMINACY - SINS OF SODOM

I come to you now confessing all my sins (name them to the LORD quietly). I confess that I have sinned against You, others and myself. I had brought shame on your name by being lazy, ignorant and disobedient to your word. I have wanted all your blessings without complying to your principals. I know that THE BLOOD OF JESUS CHRIST is for my cleansing from these sins. With your help I will begin right now to learn, and aggressively change my way of thinking and acting. I repent of all my desires for soft, easy, lazy living.

Others were involved with me in some of these sins and I now break soul ties with them. I break soul ties with these people (name them to God) with whom I have engaged in sexual vices. I also break soul ties I have made with groups that condone such actions and attitudes. I break ties with all false religions I have been in or approved of, and with movements such as the New Age Movement. I confess that I have been willingly deceived and have deceived others. I have used others for my gain. I repent of all this sin. I repent of not valuing Your Word, principals and plan for my life.

I repent of having in my possession cursed objects. I will destroy those belonging to me. I break soul ties with anyone who has dominated me. I release those that I have tried to dominate.

Because JESUS became accursed for us, we are given the opportunity to break curses and free ourselves from their effects. In THE NAME OF JESUS CHRIST, I break these curses: being a willing deceiver, disobedient to THE LORD'S COMMANDANTS, idolatry, owner's of cursed objects, house of wicked, not giving to poor, lightly esteeming parents, makers of graven images, cheating to gain property, incest, adultery, slaying the innocent for money, bestially,

homosexuals-male/female, bastards, witchcraft, those who attempt to turn anyone away from God, followers of horoscopes, failure to discipline children, abuse of children, liars, the carnal minded, sodomy, rebellion, rebellious children, nonproductivity, fugitive, vagabond, those who hate, Ahab and Jezebel, cursing parents, pride and any others in the families of effeminacy and sodomy.

I no longer will serve these demon spirits. I am a believer and I cast out these demons residing in my body in THE NAME OF JESUS CHRIST MY SAVIOUR. I command the families of effeminacy and Sodom to come out.

INCEST

Please forgive me for committing incest. Forgive me for being critical of and hating those who belong to God, are in authority over me, forced me into incest, and the sex of the rapist. Please help me with fear of adults, inability to work alone, having trouble with people in authority, not respecting others, no joy in life, and hopelessness about the future. I forgive my ancestors for their incest and I forgive the person who committed incest on me. I break the ten generation curse of incest and command the following spirits to manifest and come out of me. I command the family of incest to come out.

SINS OF THE ANCESTORS

I forgive my ancestors for creating bastards, and committing incest and sexual sins. Please forgive me for the same sins. I break the curses of the bastard, incest and sexual sins on me and my descendents. I break soul ties from being a bastard and having incest committed on me. I ask that my fragmented soul be restored. I break unnaturally close friendships, blood covenants, pacts, covenants, promises and allegiances. I command the families of sins of ancestors, and sexual sins and diseases to come out of me.

RAPE, ATTEMPTED RAPE AND SEXUAL ASSAULT

I forgive those who have abused me by rape, attempted rape or sexual assault. May God bless them with all spiritual blessings, especially salvation, bring them into all truth and meet all of their needs out of His Riches in Glory through CHRIST JESUS. I command the families of rape, attempted rape and sexual assault to come out.

SEXUAL HARASSMENT - ABUSE - ASSAULT - VIOLENCE

When I was a child or adult, whether male or female, I forgive those who have committed sexual harassment, abuse, assault and violence against me, and have given me a sexually transmitted disease. I forgive those who have committed domestic violence against me by intimidation and physical abuse especially as a woman. I forgive those for unwanted, deliberate and repeated sexual behavior: comments, gestures and touching; using sexually suggestive objects, signs,

magazines and pictures; unlawful sex discrimination and threats; forcible sexual activity, rape, fondling, incest, molestation, exhibitionism, sodomy, childhood pornography and prostitution; bribery, seductive behavior, indecent exposure; sexual touching, fondling and game playing; oral, anal and vaginal intercourse; sexual contact without consent; incest, attempted rape and unwanted sexual touch. I command the families of sexual harassment, abuse, assault and violence to come out.

SOUL TIES AND DEMONIC TIES

I pray that you would forgive me of sex with demons, rape, fornication, adultery, homosexuality, bestiality, or anything else that would cause me to have a soul tie through demonic sex. Forgive me for having demonic objects in my home or office, and for having demonic ties to them. I forgive those who would try to control me through witchcraft, parental control after marriage, control by church leaders, or anyone who would try to control my God given freewill. Forgive me for trying to control others. Forgive me for making covenants and brotherhoods, for taking oaths binding me to others, and for any unholy allegiance. Forgive me for cursing myself, family, church, nation and God.

Thank you for Godly soul ties and my covenant with you. Please strengthen Your System in my life. Help me to cleanse my soul and body, and have a right spirit. Give me spiritual strength, might and force to do your work.

We break demonic ties to parents; religions and religious leaders; tradition and cursed objects; the dead; races, colors and creeds; doctors and hospitals; and self. We now break all ungodly soul ties to humans; demonic ties to objects or animals; curses, bondage, witchcraft, bands and yokes. Command the families of soul and demonic ties, and curses to leave me.

THE CHANGE OF LIFE
For Men
I forgive my wife for problems in my life caused by the changes in her life. I ask that she forgive me for problems in her life caused by the changes in my life. Forgive me for lusting after other women and other sexual sins I have committed. Protect me from the whorish woman. Please restore me from the effects of sexual sin. I forgive Adam and Eve for the original sin and cursing mankind. Forgive me for having wrong feelings for my wife due to difficulty in having intercourse. Please heal my body so that I can have normal intercourse during my lifetime. I forgive my wife for excuses for not having sex. I command the family of change in life spirits to out.

For Women
I forgive my husband for problems in my life caused by the changes in his life. I ask that he forgive me for problems in his life caused by the changes in my life. Forgive me for lusting after other men and other sexual sins I have committed. Protect me from the whoremongering man. Please restore me from the effects of sexual sin. Forgive me for being double minded. I forgive Adam and Eve for the original sin and cursing woman kind. Forgive me for having wrong feelings for my husband due to difficulty in having intercourse. Please heal my body so that I can have normal intercourse during my lifetime. I forgive my husband for the pain of having sex. I command the family of change in life spirits to come out.

SECTION 6 - WITCHCRAFT DELIVERANCE PRAYERS

WE ASK IN THE NAME OF JESUS CHRIST, LORD, MASTER AND SAVIOR.

CONTENTS
1.   CURSES
2.   CONTACTS
3.   PRAYERS

CURSES

We break curses, spells, hexes, etc. sent upon us by enemies who seek to harm, kill or wreck havoc physically, emotionally, and spiritually. We break curses of uttering a wish of evil against one; to call for mischief or injury to fall upon; to execrate, to bring evil upon or to; to blast, vex, harass or torment with great calamities. Curses of forefathers, on prosperity, flaming darts, etc. JESUS CHRIST became a curse on the cross and blotted out the handwriting of ordinances against us. We break legal holds and remove legal grounds.

CONTACTS

We break curses of witchcraft, magic, Ouija boards and other occult games; kinds of fortune telling, palm reading, tea leaf reading, crystal balls, Tarot and other card laying; astrology, birth signs and horoscopes; the heresy of reincarnation and healing groups involved in metaphysics and spiritualism; hypnosis under any excuse or authority; rock music, including acid, hard and Jesus rock;

transcendental meditation, yoga, Zen and eastern cults and religious idol worship; martial arts, including Judo, Kung Fu and Karate; water witching or dowsing, levitation, table tipping, body lifting, psychometry (divining through objects), automatic writing and handwriting analysis; astral projection, soul and out-of-body travel, and other demonic skills; cults that deny THE BLOOD OF JESUS CHRIST and philosophies which deny THE DEITY OF THE LORD JESUS.

We renounce occult literature and will destroy such books, going to fortune tellers, reading horoscopes, believing in reincarnation, and psychic and occult contact. We break demonic holds of psychic heredity on our family line.

PRAYERS

We forgive our ancestors and others that have practiced witchcraft that would affect us. Please forgive us for practicing witchcraft. We close doors opened to Satan through contact with witchcraft, occult and similar activities. We renounce you and your kingdom.

We bind and order demons to return to senders escorted by angels to destroy seats of witchcraft. The demons are commanded to confuse, and sow terror and panic in the hearts of witches and wizards. We have power over the demons through JESUS' NAME. We command the demons to attack their works, destroy each other and to shake the kingdom of evil.

We confess as sin and renounce contact with occult, witchcraft, Satan worship and false religion, and sins of ancestors. Through ignorance, stupidity or willfulness we have sought supernatural experience apart from GOD. We forgive enemies, false prophets, diviners, liars, witches, and individuals working in concert with evil spirits and forms of spiritual activity; Satanic covens of witches and wizards; persons in witchcraft and sorcery; casting spells, potions, enchantments and curses; psychic prayers, witchcraft control, and anyone who has cursed us.

We break legal holds and grounds back to Adam and Eve. We break control, soul ties and curses. We renounce Satan and his kingdom of evil. We hate Satan, demons and evil works. We come against Water Spirits and Witchcraft Attacks In Dreams. In THE NAME OF JESUS CHRIST, LORD, MASTER AND SAVIOR, we pray and take authority over the forces of evil. We command the demons, their families and works to come out.

WE ASK IN THE NAME OF JESUS CHRIST LORD, MASTER AND SAVIOR.

CONTENTS

OVERALL PRAYER - COMMAND - WARFARE

OVERALL PRAYER

Almighty God, please forgive us for omission - commission, known - unknown, deliberate - inadvertent sins by the blood of Jesus Christ. We forgive our enemies, pray for their salvation, and break curses placed on us. We thank God for power and authority over the enemy: satan and his kingdom. We are strong in the Lord, and the power of his might. We cover us with the blood of Jesus Christ. We make a blood covenant with the father, the son, the Holy Spirit. We ask God to send our guardian angels, and an army of angels for warfare. Where God uses all and shall in the bible, we agree and declare in our lives. We use overall prayer as a preface for other prayers. We pray the Holy Bible and ask in the name of Jesus Christ: Lord, master and savior. Amen! So be it!

OVERALL COMMAND

We wrestle-bind-loose-command the kingdom of evil, all the power of the enemy, principalities, powers, rulers of darkness of this world, and spiritual wickedness in high places.

We use the power of God given to believers. We take authority over the kingdom of evil. We bind and subdue satan's empire. We enter into spiritual warfare, and assault the kingdom of darkness. We bind the forces of evil, and destroy the kingdom of evil. We send armies of warring angels to attack. We use every verse in the Holy Bible that wars against the demonic forces. We use overall command as a preface for other commands.

Overall Warfare

Concerning the work of my hands command ye me. We exercise authority over the work of God's hands. We bind and loose on earth what is bound and loosed in heaven.

We command the devil's forces to destroy each other. By the blood of Jesus Christ, we take dominion over satan. We put on the whole armour of God. We close doorways to demons. We come against the kingdom of evil. We use the word of God, written and spoken, against the forces of evil. We are the army of the Lord. We exercise dominion over nations and kingdoms. We use our tactics and weapons of war against the enemy. We return curses and weapons formed against us. We use overall warfare as a preface for other warfare.

PRAYERS AND DECLARATION

Prayer To Establish Basis For Warfare
(Intense spiritual warfare)

I forgive anyone that has had spiritual, secular or carnal authority over me including mental, physical and financial. I forgive ancestors and anyone that has hurt, cursed or controlled me. I break curses, control and soul ties brought upon me by them. I ask that God bless and forgive them, and save their souls. I set myself free from those who would hurt me.

Forgive me Lord for my many sins. I forgive myself for sinning against my body. I break curses and soul ties that I have brought upon myself. In Jesus name I pray.

Prayer Before Deliverance
(Personal deliverance or mass deliverance)

We ask God to send the Holy Spirit, the seven-fold spirit of God, warrior angels, ministering angels and twelve legions of angels. We ask the warrior angels to come with their flaming, sharp two-edged swords capable of dividing spirit and soul.

We ask God to surround us, cut off communications between the demons outside and the demons inside, and remove loose demons around us.

We bind fallen angels and demons, and loose ourselves from them. We call for spiritual warfare to set the captives free. We bind forces of evil, and loose forces of good that we have the power and authority to do so. In Jesus name I pray.

Weapons Of Warfare Declaration
(Wrestle - bind- loose - command)

Almighty God is omni (all universal): omnipotent (all power), omnipresent (all present), omniscient (all knowledge) and omnificent (all creative). He is all unlimited.

Holy! Holy! Holy! Is the Lord God almighty of righteousness and holiness, the most high God. I am, the Lord, the Lord of miracles, the supernatural God.

God of the mountains, God of eternity, God the everlasting one, God of the covenant, God of vision, God of creation, God alone eternal.

The Lord provides, the Lord sanctifies, the Lord is peace, the Lord heals, the Lord is there, the Lord God is owner.

Concerning the work of my hands command ye me. We exercise authority over the work of God's hands. We ask God of things to come concerning his sons and daughters.

We have truth, righteousness, gospel of peace, faith, salvation, sword and perseverance. We are strong, withstand, stand, quench darts, praying, watching and supplication.

We bind and loose on earth, what is bound and loosed in heaven. We restrain and destroy on earth, what is restrained and destroyed in heaven. We cast out devils in the name of Jesus Christ, and speak with new tongues by the Holy Spirit.

For we wrestle (contend & strive - engage & combat - force & move) against the kingdom of evil, all the power of the enemy, principalities, powers, the rulers of the darkness of this world and spiritual wickedness in high places. We wrestle, bind, loose and command what affects our lives, ministries and professions: evil forces of satan and fallen angels over new age, occultism, witchcraft and satanism; sexual, curses and infirmities; Christian persecution and warfare; and false doctrines and religions.

We proclaim the father, the son, the Holy Spirit and this declaration over our lives and ask God to fulfill it.

We wrestle against: (tell God what you are personally wrestling against.)

DECLARATIONS

Powerful Weapons Of Warfare
Weapons
We heal the sick, cleanse the lepers, raise the dead and cast out devils! (Matt. 10:7-8)
We bind and loose, and restrain and destroy! (Matt. 18:18)
We can do all things through Christ! (Eph. 6:10-18, Mark 9:23, Phil. 4:13, Psa. 8:6)
We can chase thousands of demons! (Deut. 32:30)
We break every yoke! (Isa. 58:6)
We strive violently into the kingdom of God! (Luke 16:16)
We will do greater works than Jesus Christ did! (John 14:12)
We are a flaming fire! (Psa. 104:4)
We command the work of God's hands! (Isa. 45:11)
We use the keys of the kingdom of heaven to open! (Matt. 16:19)
We cast out devils in the name of Jesus Christ! (Mark 16:17)
We speak with new tongues by the Holy Spirit! (Mark 16:17)
We bind and loose the power of the kingdom of evil! (Luke 10:19)
We wrestle fallen angels! (Eph. 6:12)
We have power to heal and cast out! (Mark 3:15, Luke 9:1-2)

Summaries
To root out - to pull down - to destroy - to throw down - to break:
Human nations and spiritual kingdoms! (Jer. 1:10, Jer. 51:20)
The bible: know - believe - practice. (2 Tim. 2:15, 2 Tim. 3:16, James 2:18)
Ask & receive - seek & find - knock & opened. (Matt. 7:7)
Preach - bind - open. (Isa. 61:1)
Vengeance - punishments - bind - execute. (Psa. 149:6-9)
Preach - heal - deliver - recover - liberty. (Luke 4:18)

Statements
The weapons of our warfare are mighty and powerful! (2 Cor. 10:4-5, Matt. 10:1)
God teaches our hands to war and fingers to fight! (Psa. 18:34, Psa. 144:1)
The abode of God is to be seized and the forces seized it! (Matt. 11:12)
For the word of God is quick, powerful, sharper, piercing, dividing, discerning! (Heb. 4:12)
If you don't shed the blood of the kingdom of evil, and fight against God's enemies (Satan, fallen angels and demons), you are cursed! (Jer. 48:10)
God has not changed his mind! (Ex. 22:18, Lev. 20:27)
Truly an amazing promise! What a God we serve! (Matt. 18:19)

The word of God is the sword of the spirit. (Eph. 6:17)

Proclaim the word of God.
Have childlike faith so that you can go to heaven. (Mark 10:15)
We will learn about satan's devices: wiles and intentions. (Rom. 1:13a, 2 Cor. 2:11)
The world (Including humanity and Christianity) is deceived, foolish and without understanding. (part of Rev. 12:9 , Jer. 5:21)
Every believer should be casting out devils. (Mark 16:17)
We ask God of things to come concerning his sons and daughters. (Isa. 45:11)
We do not wrestle against human beings and the demons within them. (Eph. 6:12)

Do you have a form of Godliness but deny the power? (II Tim. 3:5)
Are you following the great commission? (Mark 16:15-20)

Intense Spiritual Warfare

We command that they fall into their own traps (Snares, stumbling blocks, recompenses) that have been set for us. (Jer. 5:26)
We break soul ties to those who have practiced witchcraft and controlled us. (Gal. 5:20-21)
We return the fiery darts (Spears) and other weapons sent against us. (job 41:26, ephod. 6:16)
We turn back the weapons on those who sent them. (Isa. 54:17, Jer. 51:20, 2 Cor. 10:4)

Where they want our arms to be broken, we command that their arms to be broken. (Psa. 37:17)
Where they want to gnash out our teeth, we command that their teeth to be gnashed out. (Lam. 2:16)
Weapons (Instruments, darts, swords, handstaves, javelins, arms, quivers, bows) formed against us will not prosper. (Isa. 54:17, Jer. 51:20, 2 Cor. 10:4)

We command demons that have been sent to attack us to return and attack the senders.
We break and return curses to those who sent them.
We ask the angels to return what has been sent to attack us and to destroy witchcraft.
Every evil thing that they want to be done to us, we return and command that it be done to them.

Worldwide Spiritual Warfare
Old testament
Promises

We ask for the heathen and uttermost parts of the earth (Psa. 2:8-9).
God will break them with a rod of iron; and dash them in pieces (Psa. 2:8-9).
We ask God of things to come concerning his sons and daughters (Isa. 45:11).
We command the work of God's hands (Isa. 45:11).
God has not changed his mind (Ex. 22:18).

Commands

We have dominion! (Gen. 1:28)

We can do all things through Christ! (Psa. 8:6b)
Witchcraft will not smite us! (Psa. 121:6)
Vengeance - punishments - bind - execute! (Psa. 149:6-9)
We break every yoke! (Isa. 58:6)
To root out - to pull down - to destroy - to throw down - to break:
Human nations and spiritual kingdoms! (Jer. 1:10)
We will break in pieces the nations and destroy kingdoms! (Isa. 58:6)
We will be strong and do exploits! (Dan. 11:32b)

New Testament
Promises

Ask & receive - seek & find - knock & opened (Matt. 7:7).
We have the keys of the kingdom of heaven (Matt. 16:19).
We will do greater works than Jesus Christ did (John 14:12).
We ask for the exceeding greatness of his power (Psa. 2:8-9
We do not wrestle against human beings and the demons within them (Ephod. 6:12).
We are over the works of thy hands (Hob. 2:7-8).
Truly an amazing promise (Matt. 18:19).

We wrestle against the fallen angels.
We agree with each other according to the Holy Bible.
We ask God for the world.

Commands

We bind the strongman! (Matt. 12:29)
We bind and loose, and restrain and destroy! (Matt. 16:19)
What a God we serve! (Matt. 18:19)
We can do all things through Christ! (mark 9:23)
We bind and loose the power of the enemy, the kingdom of evil! (Luke 10:19)
Weapons (instruments, darts, swords, handstaves, javelins, arms, quivers, bows) formed against us will not prosper! (2 Cor. 10:4-5)
We turn back the weapons on those who sent them! (2 Cor. 10:4-5)
We can do all things through Christ! (Phil. 4:13)

WITCHCRAFT DELIVERANCE PRAYERS

Prayers

We forgive our ancestors and others that have practiced witchcraft affecting us. Please forgive us for practicing witchcraft. We close doors opened to satan through contact with witchcraft, new age, occultism and satanism. We renounce satan and his kingdom.

We confess contact with new age, occultism, witchcraft, satan worship, false religion. We have sought supernatural experience apart from God. We forgive enemies, false prophets, diviners, liars, witches and individuals working with evil spirits; covens of witches, warlocks and wizards; persons in witchcraft and sorcery; casting spells, potions, enchantments and curses; psychic prayers, witchcraft control and those who have cursed us.

We renounce satan and his kingdom of evil. We hate satan, demons and evil works. We come against water spirits and witchcraft attacks in dreams. In the name of Jesus Christ, Lord, master and savior, we pray and take authority over the forces of evil.

Break Curses

A curse is uttering a wish of evil against one; to call for mischief or injury to fall upon; to execrate (curse), to bring evil upon or to; to blast (violent outburst), vex (agitate), harass or torment with great calamities.

Jesus Christ became a curse on the cross and blotted out the handwriting of ordinances against us. We break curses, spells, hexes and other evil sent upon us by enemies who seek to steal, kill and destroy physically, emotionally and spiritually.

We renounce and destroy occult literature and books, going to fortune tellers, reading horoscopes, believing in reincarnation, and psychic and occult contact. We break ancestral curses, legal holds and grounds back to Adam and eve. We break control, soul ties and curses.

We break curses of witchcraft, magic, ouija boards and occult games; fortune telling, palm reading, tea leaf reading, crystal balls, tarot and card laying; astrology, birth signs and horoscopes; reincarnation; metaphysics and spiritualism; hypnosis; rock music; transcendental meditation, eastern religions; religious idol worship; yoga and martial arts; water witching and dowsing; levitation, table tipping, body lifting; psychometry (divining through objects); automatic writing; soul travel and demonic skills; denying the blood and the deity of the Lord Jesus Christ.

Commands

We bind and order demons to return to senders escorted by angels to destroy seats of witchcraft. The demons are commanded to confuse, and sow terror and panic in the hearts of witches, warlocks and wizards. We have power over the demons through Jesus' name. We command the demons to attack their works, destroy each other and shake the kingdom of evil. We command the demons, their families and works to come out.

COMMANDS AGAINST WITCHCRAFT

Natural

We proclaim, declare and agree with the holy word of God. We claim the world for the Lord.

We use the sword of the Lord to sever demonic ties (between spirits and souls, and other ties), ley lines (lines of energy / telepathic communication), and silver cords (astral projection / soul travel / bilocation) of anyone who would travel into our presence through communications, crystal balls or by their souls and spirits. We break demonic balls, cords, bowls, pitchers and wheels used against us.

We bind-restrain and loose-destroy: New Age doctrines proclaiming that self is God; you are God and I am God, denying existence of a personal God, and insisting universe itself is God:

Spiritual healing, psychics, clairvoyants, mediums and channelers; one world government / new age / occultism / witchcraft / satanism sects, cults, organizations; religious and occult philosophies; pantheism, animism, freemasonry, theosophy, illuminati, apostate Christianity, Islam, Taoism, Buddhism, Sufism, Hinduism and Babylonian pagan religions; palm reading, tarot card reading, past life therapy and spiritual counseling; demonically obtaining fame, power and money; spiritual evolution as Gods and Goddesses; and swamis, gurus, yogis, lamas, spiritual teachers.

Astrologers, mystic path, mysticism, ascetic life-style; yoga and meditation; mother earth gaia, shamanism; kundalini energy; universal oneness; worship of Lucifer and occult inner circle.

Occult knowledge; esoteric truth; ancient mysteries; the Christ; Luciferian age of Aquarius; the plan; the great work of ages; world servers; Masonic religion of evolution; divine aspects of man; and dark magic arts. Included are demonic practices of new age - occultism - witchcraft - satanism.

Supernatural

We bind and cast down strongmen and strongholds (satan, angels and demons) over new age, occultism, witchcraft, satanism and demonic arts: principalities, powers, rulers of darkness of this world, spiritual wickedness in high places; might, kingdoms, thrones, dominions, nobles, princes, kings; ascended masters, spirit guides; mind control, mind occult, mind binding; witchcraft, sorcery, divination, necromancy; eastern mysticism, reincarnation, transcendental meditation, soul travel; martial arts, yoga; visualization, demonic inner healing; familiars; crystal helpers; bodiless spheres of light; and universal intelligence.

Reversal

We reverse satanic supernatural power against Christians from demonic prayers, blasphemy (contempt), execration and imprecations (cursing), invocations (conjuring), profanity (language), and retributions (punishment). We reverse harm, affliction, injury, evil and misfortune.

Made in the USA
Las Vegas, NV
10 March 2025

19330796R00031